© Mitha & Associés, 2016

Printed by CreateSpace.

ISBN: 978-1518653452

Nila Mitha

Finance
for non-financials:
an introduction

Follow the growth of a business step by step:
from startup to development

Foreword

Remember how as kids we were all taught some money lessons?

As far as I am concerned, I was taught my first lesson when I was four years old. Back from a great day at school I asked my entrepreneurial parents if I could be rewarded for it: they showed me the empty cash drawer and explained that they would only be able to do so once they had sold something and received some money in exchange!

A case of cash shortage that led to my first lesson in business finance!

Finance for non-financials: an introduction

Note to the reader

In order to introduce you to business and business finance in a practical and lively fashion, I have chosen a cleaning company whose business is easy to understand, as an example. In fact, the issues managers are faced with when running a business are all similar, regardless of business type.

This book, as you will have realized, is not about the cleaning business.

A service-based business is a good starting point to learn about finance and understand the issues at stake more easily.

Furthermore please note that assumptions concerning the rate of social security contributions, company taxes and duties correspond to the French averages and legal context.

Test your business knowledge

1. A 5% increase in sales corresponds to an equivalent capacity to increase salaries.

– True

– False

2. There are different margins level ratios in a business.

– True

– False

3. A company's net income can be a profit or a loss.

– True

– False

4. Profits earned by a company do not automatically result in an increase in cash flow.

– True

– False

5. The difference between profit and cash generated by the company is only tied to dividend payments.

– True

– False

6. Cash flow generated from the company's operating activities will help determine if the company has the means to invest and to comply with loan repayment terms.

– True

– False

7. If company expenses increase by 3% and sales by 2% its income will improve.

– True

– False

8. EBITDA is the operational indicator of performance that is most frequently used. EBITDA gives the company leeway to invest or finance its business.

– True

– False

9. If client payment terms are extended, the impact on cash flow will be negative.

– True

– False

10. If supplier payment terms are extended, the impact on cash flow will be temporarily favorable.

– True

– False

See annex for answers page 123

Introduction

According to the World Bank there are 125 million formal SMEs (up to 250 employees) in the 132 countries covered by the study out of which 89 million operate in emerging markets.

More and more people around the world and even more so amongst the Millennium generation, wish to become entrepreneurs. According to the last E&Y 2015 survey, 65 % of young people are willing to start their own business. In this context it is key to master the main business financial concepts and basics.

You will wonder, why another book on finance for non-financials? There are so many already available on the market and even for free on the web sites!

Most of the books cover the same topic with a very theoretical approach and will leave you with the idea that business finance is the exclusive domain of experts.

This book is not about accounting or bookkeeping: it is about understanding the impact of business operations on the financial statements.

Therefore I have decided to take you through the entrepreneurship venture from a financial point of view and by following Anna and Martin through the development stages of the startup and the first five years of their "AM-Clean"business.

The book also covers the struggles of the SME's shareholders and management to find financing and grow their business while taking into account that most government policies are tailored for large corporations and not for small businesses.

When I was Chief Financial Officer I noticed that many executives and operations staff in non-finance functions did not master the basics of finance and yet were expected to improve the company performance!

How could they sell, purchase or innovate if they did not understand how their actions would impact profits and cash and how could we expect them to align management and shareholders objectives? I therefore decided to introduce training sessions on finance for all the non-finance teams and the result was impressive:

- Financial objectives were more easily shared and understood.

- Communication with finance teams on monthly results was facilitated.

- Company performance improved.

Since I started my own consulting firm, I have met many managers and entrepreneurs who are faced with various issues when they have to transform their vision, strategy and actions into financials or when they need to discuss with potential investors or banks. This book will help them talk the same language and communicate with the resources providers more efficiently.

When I teach finance, either in business schools or to non-finance executives I start by telling them that we are all using finance reasoning without knowing it! Let's discover how.

1

We are all entrepreneurs
without knowing it

Wouldn't you say that our personal financial situation bears several similarities to a business situation?

In fact, in order to have a greater understanding of a business and its respective challenges let us try to analyze the economic behavior of a household throughout the major stages of its life cycle.

Paul and Lisa completed their studies and after spending time as interns and unemployed, they both obtained permanent work contracts and were therefore able to rent an apartment. They decided to start a family, which we will call the Family company.

1. The Family company settles into an active working life with the following objectives in mind:

- Furnish and equip their home, i.e. *invest* by using savings they have set aside and by taking out a bank loan i.e. find *financing*.

- Spend, while balancing income and expenses, i.e. manage their cash flow or cash.

2. The Family plans to grow, so it analyzes its annual financial results and prepares a provisional budget in order to:

- Save up to welcome a baby.

- Balance the budget taking into account a *savings* objective i.e. generate a surplus or make a profit in order to be able to save: they will build a strategy to increase their borrowing capacity.

- Find the best means of making a safe investment and watch their savings grow. The Family Company is not happy with the interest rates offered by a savings account but after looking around for a better option they accept it because:

  – it is a risk-free investment with a guaranteed return on savings;

  – funds are not blocked so they are available when and as needed.

In fact, the Family company had initially considered investing their savings in shares of a reputable listed company as it offered a *higher return rate (dividend) than a savings account* but with a risk of capital loss, if at the time of the share sale, the value of the chosen share had gone down.

This helped the Family company understand why as shareholders they would have asked for a dividend in return for their investment at a rate higher than that of the interest rate of a savings account. This helped the Family company understand why as shareholders they would have asked for a Return On Investment (ROI) that was higher than the interest rate on a savings account. *This difference in rate corresponds to the risk premium.*

3. Lisa and Paul have both advanced in their careers and achieved their professional goals with promotions and salary increases.

Their earnings have grown, and the Family Company has increased its *revenue* and they now have 2 kids, which leads to the decision to purchase a home.

Let's review their financial plan:

- *Thanks to the sound management of its budget, the Family was able to achieve a budgetary surplus i.e. an annual profit: it therefore generated a financing capacity in order to obtain a loan, which will help to finance its investment.*

- The Family reviews its budget based on current tax regulations as it has become liable to pay income tax – is it looking at tax optimization? It has to include new areas of expenditure: *repayment of the loan, interest expenses and taxes.*

- In order to become homeowners, Paul and Lisa had to move further away from their workplace. They will therefore have to employ a domestic worker (child care) for 3 hours a day, who will pick up the children at school and look after them until the parents come home.

4. The Family has at last found a property to buy but a new tax rule has disrupted their development plans:

- Interest on a mortgage for the purchase of a primary residence is no longer tax deductible.

- The Family reviews its budget and will have to either continue saving or reducing its operating costs such as its winter vacation…It chooses to start a savings plan in order to adjust to the tax change.

It is clear that *fiscal instability* does not only affect companies but also the investment choices and decisions of the Family company.

5. The Family has adjusted well to its new situation but unfortunately the financial health of Paul's company has deteriorated and the management team is considering a restructuring plan so Paul will lose his job.

The Family must once again adjust to a new economic situation by restructuring family expenses and by setting priorities to maintain spending on the children's personal development (e.g. sports and culture).

The Family's restructuring plan will focus on two cost items:

- *make the choice to divest by giving up the second car;*
- *reduce running costs by dismissing the domestic worker.*

6. The Family company is on the road to recovery, social buffers such as unemployment benefits and the training program proposed to Paul have enabled him to find a new job and make a new business plan.

By following this admittedly simplified outline of the Family company's financial activity we can begin to understand a normal company's business-related issues: are not the actions and objectives of the two identical and possible options and decisions similar?

We are all set to try and understand the challenges a business faces and what drives its decisions.

2

The business project

Let's take a look at Anna and Martin's case. After having worked in the same company they are now going through a professional transition, in other words they are unemployed.

They have kept in touch and are considering creating a new company providing cleaning services for factories and offices in their area. They have work experience in similar companies, believe in their business project and have even presented it to potential clients who have shown a keen interest in it. One of the clients is ready to sign a contract as soon as they start the business.

For this particular client the closure of the previous cleaning company had entailed extra costs, as the factory had to readjust to another service provider who proposed inadequate working hours for his factory and was situated 100 kilometers (more than 60 miles) away.

It's an industry that Anna and Martin are familiar with. After spending 10 years in the same company, Anna as sales manager and Martin as financial controller, they have both decided to venture into entrepreneurship.

They are looking forward to the challenge of starting their own business: at this moment in time is it their goal to become rich?

No, their main motivation is the desire to be their own boss in order to avoid being laid off: a need for greater independence and why not, contribute to the development of their region by creating jobs…

Wanting to earn more money comes a distant fourth in their list of motivations.

They also know that (in France):

- They will have to use their personal savings as capital contribution for the company in question. As far as Anna is concerned, if the company runs into difficulties during the course of its business life she will have to use the studio she owns as collateral.

- 35% of new companies never make it beyond their third year.

- Their average working week will be around 50 hours and often much more during the first years; their annual leave will also be reduced (and that's if they can take any leave at all!).

- The average salary for small business managers with less than 20 employees will probably peak at a monthly net income of about €4 250 and that's after several years in business.

- As company directors they are legally liable for their company.

After having considered all the difficulties facing an entrepreneur, and with the support of a potential client, they decide to turn their project into reality.

Anna and Martin start by writing a *business plan*, which is a document that describes the business project as a whole and consists of several sections: the business, the market analysis, the marketing strategy, human resources etc. The financial section must include at the very least an income statement, a cash-flow statement as well as a balance sheet over 3 to 5 years.

The purpose of the business plan is to first and foremost validate the feasibility of the project, chart a course and outline the steps that need to be taken. Actual results will be compared with the plan month after month.

It also serves to convince potential partners, investors, and financial institutions to provide the financial needs outlined in the business plan.

Anna and Martin have defined the structure of their company and their respective roles: Anna will be the Chief Executive Officer (CEO) and main shareholder; she has a thorough knowledge of the market and is well acquainted with her potential clients' needs. Martin will be the Administrative and Financial Director, and will support Anna with strategic planning and its implementation.

Martin suggests that Anna enroll in a beginner's course in business finance so that she can make operational decisions consistent with the company's financial objectives, be able to defend the pricing strategy as well as feel confident during negotiations with the various stakeholders.

While Anna follows her training program, Martin will finalize the financial section of the business plan.

3

The business environment

Martin enrolled Anna in a "finance course for non-financials" so let's follow along.

On the first day, we are going to learn the business finance terminology with Anna, and try to understand what it means so that we can find our way through the accounts.

A company is not an island solely governed by its management and shareholders: it is part and parcel of an economic environment operating in a given legal and regulatory framework and with partners that we shall call stakeholders.

Who are these stakeholders and what do they do?

1. The majority shareholders

The company directors that we are going to follow are majority shareholders, i.e. they hold more than 50% of the company shares, which is the case for most of the small and medium-sized companies. Their duties are as follows:

• Mobilize resources such as money from investors, obtain bank loans, and rally other stakeholders including employees.

• Pay resources providers.

• Attract clients in a competitive market and generate profitable sales.

• Lead the company to sustainable prosperity.

2. The minority shareholders

In our particular case they are represented by Anna and Martin's friends, who firmly believe in the business project and are ready to invest their personal savings. What can they expect in exchange? To earn higher returns than with their savings account but also to accept the double risk that they might not cash in dividends for at least 5 years or that they might lose their investment.

The amount invested by the shareholders can be found in the company's share capital as ownership interest) on the liability side of the balance sheet (what the company owes to the shareholders!) and balanced on the assets side as an entry of an equivalent amount (what the company owns) identified as cash at bank. The capital is part of the company's resources. This capital that was deposited in a bank account when the company was created will be used to cover the startup and development expenses.

3. The employees

Employees participate in the running of the company: they are bound by an employment contract and are paid in exchange for the work they provide.

The related salaries and social security contributions can be found in the company's income statement (profit and loss account) under operating expenses.

4. The suppliers

We can distinguish three main categories of suppliers who also contribute to the running of the company and are paid for the goods and services:

• Non-current assets suppliers: property, manufacturing equipment, transport, various installations such as factory and office layouts, the IT system etc., which will enable to produce the goods and services sold.

These are called fixed assets or non-current assets, as they will be in use for several years (3 to 20 years) and transferred on an annual basis to the income statement as depreciation.

When a company acquires material it will use for an estimated minimum of 5 years, only a fifth of the purchase price will be allocated in the first year, the rest will be allocated over the following four financial years.

Thus, we can find on the assets side of the balance sheet (the fixed assets) at its purchase price value and at its net value after deducting the accumulative depreciation at the end of the accounting period. On the other hand the annual depreciation will be reported as a depreciation expense in the income statement.

- Trade suppliers: raw materials, goods and services to process during the production cycle and to sell.

  They can be found on the company's income statement under expenses, which are considered as cost of goods and services sold, and on the balance sheet as inventory of raw material, work in progress or finished products...

- Other trade suppliers: overhead costs such as rent, insurance, advertising, travel expenses etc.

  Overheads can be found on the company's income statement under operating costs, detailed by nature of expenses.

In general suppliers are paid between 45 and 60 days. These payment terms serve to offset the payment terms granted to clients.

In the interim, unpaid amounts (including taxes) of accounts payable (trade payables) are entered on the balance sheet under current liabilities.

5. The clients

They are the key to the company's success. In order to buy the goods and services offered by the company, clients expect quality products at competitive prices in exchange, i.e. within the same price range proposed by local and international competitors for the same products and services.

The customers are shown on the income statement as revenue. In general this revenue should cover company expenses and thus reach a breakeven point (level where company sales equal expenses).

If sales are less than expenses, the company shows operating losses: this would be the same as income that is less than expenses as shown in our previous example of Paul and Lisa's Family business.

In general the company grants clients 45-day payment terms and while invoices remain unpaid, they are accounted for on the assets side of the balance sheet with the amounts including sales taxes under the heading *trade receivables*.

6. Banks and credit institutions

They generally perform 3 functions:

- They provide long-term financing resources, mainly to finance investments (fixed assets) intended for the development of the company.

  In return they receive an interest rate that depends on the money market, plus a few additional percentage points depending on the estimated risk. The risk varies depending on the quality of the business project, operating performance potential and its ability to generate cash and repay its loans.

- They can provide short and middle term financing via overdraft facilities or factoring (advances on accounts receivable).

- They manage the company's cash flows (bank account, transfers, checks etc.) and propose short-term investments to optimize cash flow management.

Information concerning financing can be found on these two statements:

– on the company's income statement for the interest paid;

– on the liabilities side of the balance sheet under long term or short (current) term financial debts (liabilities) for the outstanding loan amount.

If the company has cash available it can be found on the assets side of the balance sheet under current assets (banks, cash and cash equivalent.

7. The Government

The Government allows all business stakeholders to run the business in a given setting (within a set framework) in compliance with company laws, labor laws, tax laws etc. It also provides general infrastructures such as the education system, social security, power networks, roads, airports and so on.

In return, the government and government agencies levy social security contributions and taxes and grant, depending on the business sector, reductions in employment costs, tax credits, subsidies etc.

They appear on the income statement classified by nature of expenses (taxes, social contributions, income taxes) or other revenue (subsidies, tax credits). On the balance sheet they can be identified as other current liabilities or other current assets.

For SMEs the complex rules and regulations as well as frequent amendments are administrative burdens that have an impact on costs that are not immediately visible. These invisible costs most often dealt with by the manager himself make it difficult to concentrate on the running of the company.

Amendments to existing rules and regulations and changes for calculating various taxes result in real additional costs, as it is necessary to adapt the company's software (invoicing, payroll, accounting etc.) and pay for consulting services constantly.

8. Competitors

In order to understand its market and products thoroughly, the company has to identify its competitors; analyze their strengths and weaknesses, be capable of embracing innovation and be able to offer prices that are acceptable in the marketplace and are competitive.

Pricing is a direct result of costs necessary to produce the goods or services plus operating cost (overheads) and the addition of a percentage of expected profit margin that will among other things be used to pay new investments, taxes, shareholders.

Competitors have no direct impact on the company's accounts but being in a weak position in relation to competitors, i.e. in a non-competitive product-quality and or value-for-money situation, sales will be the first affected.

In fact, if the company cannot sell its services or goods because it is not competitive enough it cannot expect to generate a profit.

9. Employee representatives

In order to foster good working relationships, relations with trade union and employee representatives must be based on trust and transparency and not on a permanent power struggle between stakeholders such as in France.

These relationships do not have a direct impact on the company's accounts as such, but due to the complexity of the labor code, managing industrial relations can incur significant costs in terms of time and expertise.

At the end of the first day Anna feels a bit lost and wonders how she can keep up with the next two days of the course. She knows that she needs to have a better understanding of resources (source of funds) and use of funds, so she asks the teacher to summarize the lesson:

1. Company resources presented as liabilities on the balance sheet correspond to the means at its disposal to obtain assets:

- Cash contributed by the shareholders (capital) and possibly by credit institutions (loans).

- Suppliers that will provide the raw materials, goods and other services.

- Employees (human resources) who will work on producing and selling the goods or services.

2. Use of funds presented as assets on the balance sheet correspond to what the company owns after using the resources at its disposal:

- Intangible assets (licenses, leaseholds, brands etc.) and tangible assets (property, materials etc.) that will serve to produce the goods or services.

- Stocks (inventories) of raw materials, work in progress meant for production (if it is a manufacturing company) or merchandise to sell (if it is a distribution company).

- Trade receivables and other receivables.

- Cash and cash equivalent available.

4

The financial mechanism

Reassured by her teacher's encouraging comments and having understood the principles of assets and liabilities, source and use of funds, as well as income and expenses, Anna is ready to take on the next two days of training.

We are now going to discover how to evaluate the company's business performance with Anna.

The company raises capital that it invests to create wealth that will be used to pay its resource providers (including shareholders) and to finance its development.

In order to ensure its sustainability, the company has to enter a virtuous cycle that creates value and should be able to face the challenges of downward cycles and cyclical crises.

As a consequence of this virtuous cycle the company performs well, that is to say generates long-term positive results and cash flow.

The company's ability to do so, coupled with the credibility of its management is evaluated by a credit institution like a bank for example, before granting short term or long term loans.

An employee who wishes to join a company or any other stakeholder can verify its financial position beforehand by obtaining the company accounts from the commercial court registry, if the company is registered. This possibility can vary from country to country, but if the company is listed on a stock exchange then its financial reports can be found on the company website.

The three major financial statements – income statement (profit and loss account), statement of cash-flows and statement of financial position (balance sheet) are reported by companies in accordance with the GAAP (principles defined by each country), which tend to converge with international standards such as IFRS (International Financial Reporting Standards) in Europe or US GAAP.

Now let's see what this is all about?

These statements contain information concerning 2 consecutive financial years (2014 & 2015).

In each of these statements, we can identify the elements that apply to:

- The company's operating cycle.
- Its investment policy.
- Its financial strategy.

Let's find out more:

1. The income statement

The income statement measures the profit or loss for the financial period and is obtained by subtracting expenses from sales and other income.

The income statement records all revenues and expenses for a given accounting period (12 months maximum according to accounting rules) classified in a particular order, and enabling the calculation of intermediate subtotals called performance indicators.

4.1 Simplified Income Statement or Profit and Loss Account

	Sales (turnover)
	- Cost of Sales
	= Gross Margin
Operating	- Overheads
	- Personnel Cost
	- Social Charges
	= EBITDA
Investing	- Depreciation and Provisions
	= EBIT
Financing	+/- Interest expenses or Income
	= EBT
Net Income or Loss Transferred to the Balance Sheet	+/- Non Recurring Items
	- Corporate Income Tax
	= Net Income or Loss

EBITDA: *Earnings Before Interest, Taxes, Depreciation and Amortization*
EBIT: *Earnings Before Interest and Taxes*
EBT: *Earnings Before Taxes.*

What can we find on an income statement?

In an income statement we can distinguish several levels of information concerning the business activity:

a. Sales

Total sales are the first indicator that shows whether a business has a target market, has clients and if its business is growing, stable or decreasing.

b. Gross Margin

It is a key indicator for a company that produces or distributes goods as one can find the production costs or costs of goods sold. Gross margin is the difference between sales revenue and cost of goods sold.

In a service industry, gross margin ratio to sales is very high and will vary sharply in a company producing or distributing goods, based on how much processing is required for the products sold.

Gross margin should cover all the other company costs.

c. EBITDA (Earnings before interest, taxes, depreciation and amortization)

EBITDA is the balance obtained by the difference between the gross margin and operating costs such as salaries, contributions, taxes and overheads. In other words EBITDA is equal to operating revenue minus operating expenses.

EBITDA measures the company's operating performance before taking into account the following elements:

– Depreciation (amount of non-current assets spread over the period);

– Financing costs, i.e. interest on borrowing (loans).

It is a key indicator of the company's financial performance, which is used to compare performance between companies and for business valuation.

It also serves to measure the company's gross capacity to generate cash for investments and financing.

And finally it serves to prepare the statement of cash-flow.

d. EBIT (Earnings before interest and taxes)

EBIT measures the company's performance after deducting the impact of depreciation charges on fixed assets, provisions for write-downs of inventory (devaluation of stocks) or provisions for depreciation of trade receivables as well as goodwill amortization.

These depreciations and provisions reported on the income statement do not have a direct impact on cash flow.

The acquisition or disposal of non-current assets (capital expenditure) or the non-collection of a trade receivable or sales of goods or finished products at a reduced value will have an impact on cash flow.

e. EBT (Earnings before tax)

It measures the company's performance after deducting financing costs for short or long-term loans and adding financial products if any.

f. Net income

Net income is obtained after deducting extraordinary items such as profit or loss on the sale of significant investments (subsidiaries, manufacturing plants) or restructuring costs and corporate income taxes.

Note that in France a mandatory bonus scheme "participation aux bénéfices" for companies having more than 50 employees is in force. It takes into account defined calculation rules and is reported after the EBT.

Net income corresponds to profit or loss generated by the company during the given financial period. After closing the year-end accounts, net income is transferred to the balance sheet and will increase or decrease shareholder's equity.

2. Statement of cash flows

The cash-flow statement presents how the company generated or consumed cash during the same financial period as the income statement (e.g. 2015 financial year).

It takes into account variations in the amount of inventories, receivables, payables, share capital and long-term financing as well as acquisition or divestment of non-current assets.

The company's ability to generate cash relies on:

- Its operating performance, i.e. to deliver a positive EBITDA result.
- Effective management of the operating cycle (cash conversion cycle), i.e. estimating the working capital needs for the time it takes to convert cash requirements into cash returns.
- Its investment policy.
- Its financing strategy.

4.2 Simplified Cash Flow Statement

Operating	EBITDA
	Corporate Tax
	Financial Interest or Income
	Working Capital Variance

1. Cash Flow from Operating Activities (Used or Generated)

2. Cash Flow from Investing Activities:
Purchase or Sale of Non Current Assets

3. Free Cash Flow = **1** + **2**

Financing	Share Capital Increase
	Long Term Financial Debts
	Dividends Paid

4. Cash Flow from Financing Activities

Net Cash (Used or Generated) = **3** + **4**

What is the purpose of the cash-flow statement?

After analyzing the income statement, we can see if the company generated cash or if on the contrary it used (consumed) cash. It can also help to understand the causes thereof.

a. Net cash from operating activities

It is obtained by adding expenses and financial income for the financial period, corporate taxes and changes in working capital needs between two consecutive periods to EBITDA.

It represents the operating elements that have an impact on cash flow.

Depreciation does not have an impact on cash flow. It's a method of allocating the cost of a capital expenditure (a piece of equipment) over its useful life of five years. *It is the purchase of the equipement that triggers net cash outflow.*

Working Capital requirements (WC) are calculated using the following formula:

$$WC = \frac{\text{Inventory} + \text{Trade Receivables} + \text{Other Receivables}}{- \text{Trade Payables} - \text{Other Payables}}$$

Funds needed for a complete sales cycle can be measured by calculating working capital requirements: a company has to first finance the purchase or the production of goods or services before making them available for sale. Afterwards the customer will, in general, pay 45 days after the sale has taken place.

Companies that receive cash payments from clients (e.g. supermarkets) finance their businesses by using the credit gap before suppliers have to be paid.

Calculating working capital requirements is a key element for a company's cash management: it can determine the amount required to finance the company's operating activity, at a given point in time.

In the early years of a business, a proper estimation and a thorough understanding of working capital needs are essential as banks rarely finance working capital needs except through specific products that are not always accessible to a young company.

To calculate the cash generated by operating activities as at 31/12/2015, the changes in working capital over two periods (e.g. 31/12/2014 and 31/12/2015) have to be taken into account.

For a growing business, the changes will be positive and will lead to additional cash being consumed.

It is easier to analyze and understand these changes, if they are calculated item by item between the two periods.

For example, if the accounts receivable increased between the two periods, this change will have a negative impact on cash flow; if on the contrary it decreased, there will be a positive impact on the cash flow.

But it is important to understand these impacts correctly.

In fact, a decrease in accounts receivable can mean several things; either the customers paid within a shorter time period than the previous year and that would mean cash flow was generated for a good reason or it could mean that it is lower due to a decrease in revenue for the period.

Anna does not understand the impact of these variations too well. The teacher suggests creating a summary report that can be used as a reference table!

Working Capital Items	Changes between two Periods	Cash Flow Impact
Inventory, Receivables	Increase	**Negative** Burnt / Used
	Decrease	**Positive** Generated
Payables	Increase	**Positive** Generated
	Decrease	**Negative** Burnt / Used

All other working capital items can be analyzed in this way.

b. Cash flow generated or consumed (used) by investments

For a company that invests, cash flow from investments presents a negative balance and corresponds to cash used by the business.

The report shows the overall cost of acquiring assets such as industrial facilities, manufacturing materials, office and computer equipment etc., needed to produce the company's goods and services.

If the company acquires another company as part of its development, the cost will be reported in the statement. If on the contrary it sells fixed assets, the sale price will be included in the balance.

A company divests when it sells assets that are obsolete or when its sells non-strategic assets during a restructuring period in order to renew its manufacturing assets or when it sells a subsidiary (financial non-current assets).

c. Net cash from (used in) financing activities

This last balance helps us to understand how the company either financed the cash outflows generated by the operating cycle and the investment cycle or used cash generated by these same cycles.

This balance shows respectively, cash contributions from shareholders when the company was created or share capital increased, long-term financing and successive repayments as well as dividend payments.

d. Net cash-flow generated or used during the period

The sum of the above three accounts' figures provides insight into whether the company has generated or consumed cash during the given period.

We can find the net cash flow generated by the company during a certain period by calculating the difference between the net cash available that is shown on the balance sheet between two periods.

3. The balance sheet

The company's balance is a snapshot of the company's financial situation presented as of the last day of the reporting period. All

4.3 Simplified Statement of Financial Position

Assets	=	Liabilities
Investing (Non Current Assets)		**Financing**
Fixed Assets	Total	Share Capital
Financial Assets	Net Equity	Reserves
	or	Retained Earnings
	Owners' Equity	Net Income or Loss
Operating (Current Assets)		
Inventories		Financial Debts (Long Term)
Trade Receivables		
Other Debtors		Short term fiancial debts
		Overdraft
Cash and Cash equivalent		
		Operating (Current Liabilities)
		Trade Payables
		Other Creditors

the company's sources of financing can be found in the liabilities section and how they were used in the assets section.

The balance sheet will help us to understand:

- The company's financial history: if we look at the shareholder's equity we can see the amount invested by the shareholders and the accumulated undistributed profits or losses since the company was created.

- The type of business: the proportion and detail of fixed assets will indicate if it owns licenses, patents, factories, offices etc. The type of inventory (raw materials, work in progress, finished goods) will help us to define the type of industry: industry with a long production cycle (construction companies, railways, aeronautics etc.), industries with a short production cycle (textiles, parts, everyday consumer products (staple products), or service industries.

- If operating assets (accounts receivable) can cover operating liabilities (accounts payable).

- If the company has sufficient cash to repay loans and/or to invest or if it shows a net debt position.

After having analyzed the income statement and the cash-flow statement what other information can we find on the balance sheet?

Let's have a look at the elements that make up a balance sheet.

a. Liabilities

- Net equity is made up of the capital invested by shareholders since the company was created, by undistributed profits or accumulated losses since the company was created.

These assets and liabilities are classified under several headings in the company's balance sheet:

– Retained earnings: includes the balance of undistributed net earnings or previous accumulated losses;

– The net result (income) that corresponds to the 2015 financial year as at 31/12/2015.

Net equity is one of the company's performance indicators. It serves as a reference for investors and lenders such as banks. The level of net equity is an indication of the company's capacity to obtain a long-term loan.

The company's net equity also represents the company's benchmark value, which is used to estimate its value in the event of a sale or the entry of new shareholders.

Long-term liabilities represent all the long-term financing obtained by the company. They are reduced by the annual repayments that can be found on the cash-flow statement. The debt ratio will have an impact on the company's future cash flow: the loan repayments will consume cash flow generated by the operating activity.

In general provisions correspond to sums set aside for probable future risks (litigation employee claims, commercial claims, restructuring costs etc.) as well as provisions for compensations and benefits (this account entry will depend on the accounting principles used by the company).

These provisions will have an impact on the company's cash flow in the future.

• Overdrafts or financial debts (liabilities) payable within one year: in general when a company does not have available cash-flow equal to at least its short term financial debts, one can say that the company has had cash-flow problems and that it is in an overdraft position.

In this case, we must try to understand if the overdraft is simply due to a difficult phase or if it is a harbinger of financial problems in the near future.

- Other liabilities such as debts related to the company's operating cycle such as suppliers, social security debts (paid leave and social security contributions or fiscal debts (payable VAT -sales tax- and income taxes).

Please note, when liabilities increase it is either a sign of an increase in business activity, which is a positive sign or difficulty in paying suppliers within the agreed deadlines.

It should also be noted that certain companies use their accounts payable (trade payables) to adjust their cash flow. It is unethical to burden business partners with the company's difficulties. This type of adjustment is used in particular during the closing of a financial period in order to publish « good results ».

A company whose trade accounts payable (supplier item) has disproportionately increased in comparison to the growth of the business activity could be showing signs of cash-flow issues.

b. Assets

- Fixed assets or non-currents assets represent all investments made by the company in order to produce goods or services.

The following can be found:

– intangible assets if the company has purchased licenses, patents, brands;

- tangible assets at cost less depreciation such as property, industrial facilities, tools, premises, office equipment and so on.
- land, which cannot be depreciated, is carried at acquisition cost.

A company is said to be highly capital-intensive when its business activity requires the acquisition of numerous and costly fixed assets (construction companies, production plants etc.)

A company, whose business is the transport of goods, will classify its vehicles as tangible assets if they have been purchased. If on the other hand its business is selling transport vehicles they will be entered under inventory.

The level of accumulated depreciation of tangible assets indicates the level of obsolescence of the company's assets. If the industrial facilities have depreciated by more than 50 % this could mean that the company will need to make the necessary investments to renew its facilities in the years to come and therefore will have to forecast cash requirements (financing) to that effect.

A low level of depreciation signifies that the company owns relatively new equipment: it has used (consumed) cash in previous years or in the current year.

- Financial assets represent deposits and guarantees paid by the company for office rental and opening various accounts. Significant amounts can correspond to shareholdings in other companies and subsidiaries. They form part of the non-current assets.

- Inventory represents products purchased and destined for resale or for production by the company. It can include raw materials: works in progress, finished manufactured goods or finished goods. A consultancy company or a services provider will not have significant amounts of inventory on its balance sheet.

An increase in the level of inventory is either a sign of business growth or a decrease in the business activity. Inventory can be measured according to the level of activity, production process or delivery terms. A company that has an unusually high level of inventory has tied up cash.

A business that sells 100 articles per month and has over 300 articles in inventory, i.e. three months' worth of sales will have used up cash unnecessarily.

Reasons, which may justify a high level of inventory, are the necessity to have a backup stock to compensate for uncertain delivery dates and to respect the minimum quantities called for by the supplier.

• Operating receivables: they represent accounts receivable (trade receivables) and tax receivables (deductible VAT reimbursed by the fiscal authorities.

A level of accounts receivable that is on the increase compared to the previous period could mean sales growth and/or an extension of payment deadlines to clients, which will have an unfavorable impact on cash flow.

On the contrary, a level of accounts receivable that decreases could be due to a decrease in activity or a reduction in clients' payment deadlines.

• Cash and cash equivalent represent the sum of bank balances available, and short-term investments.

Net cash position (Net cash available) is the sum of cash available on the assets side, minus the amount of possible overdrafts on the liabilities side.

This is what financiers often call a company's « war chest ».

Companies that have significant cash reserves available, superior to their annual capacity to generate net cash will have the means to invest in their future developments, handle a temporary crisis, or offer better dividends to shareholders.

c. Main balance sheet equations

4.4 **Main Balance Sheet Equations**

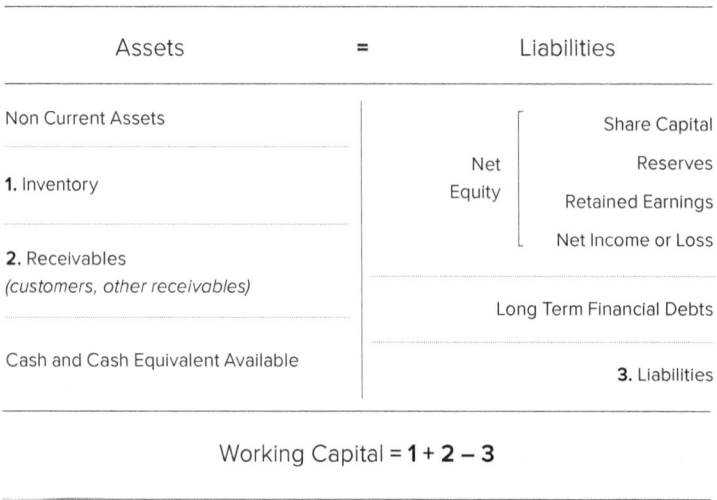

Assets	=	Liabilities
Non Current Assets		Share Capital
	Net	Reserves
1. Inventory	Equity	Retained Earnings
		Net Income or Loss
2. Receivables (customers, other receivables)		Long Term Financial Debts
Cash and Cash Equivalent Available		**3.** Liabilities

Working Capital = **1** + **2** − **3**

The balance sheet format based on the double-entry accounting principle contains some equations that can help us understand the basic structure of a business: funds posted as liabilities are equal to the use the company has made of these funds.

Assets = Liabilities

In other words the assets correspond to what the company owns and the liabilities correspond to what the company owes.

Assets − Liabilities = Net Equity (Owners Interest)

Assets = Net Equity + Liabilities (Current and Non Current)

These equations provide information concerning the financing structure of assets.

Operating Assets - Operating Liabilities
= Working Capital

It is the amount required to finance the company's operating activity, at a given point in time.

3. Overview of the 3 financial statements

In order to analyze or understand the company's financial statements it is advisable to examine and compare them over 2 periods (e.g. 31/12/2014 and 31/12/2015), which will provide some elements of comparison.

A company's performance cannot be measured with results obtained over one single period: in order to understand the results obtained end of December 2015, it is also necessary to examine the results end of December 2014.

In general, financing providers such as credit institutions analyze the financial statements over a minimum period of 3 years in order to gain a thorough understanding of a company's performance.

The financial statements are analyzed as follows: variations in value and percentage, ratios to sales or to total expenses in sales, for the income statement, contribution in percentage of balance sheet items to total assets or a combination of certain elements for a deeper analysis.

The cash-flow statement will provide a basic understanding on how the cash was generated or used with the identification of the 3 subtotals.

The three financial statements are issued on the same date (12/31/2015) and directly linked by two elements:

• Profits (or losses) for the financial period are transferred to the balance sheet and contribute to either an increase or a decrease in net equity for a given period.

• Net cash generated or consumed during the financial period will increase or decrease the amount of cash available at the previous closing date.

Now that Anna's course has ended, she is ready to join Martin who will show her the financial section of the business plan. Before that, her teacher would like her to briefly explain the type of information that can be found on each of the three financial statements:

• On the income statement we can find details of the company's sales and other income and expenses (cost of goods sold, salaries, social security contributions, overhead costs) for the financial year (2015) and determine whether the company made a profit or a loss.

- The balance sheet provides a snapshot of what the company owns, (assets) and what it owes (liabilities) at a given point in time (12/31/2015).

- The cash-flow statement can be consulted to find out if the company generated or consumed cash during the 2015 financial period. This statement also provides information concerning the elements that contributed towards consuming or generating cash.

There are two key relationships between the income statement, the cash-flow statement and the balance sheet. They provide an understanding of the company's financial situation or at least the trend reflected over two consecutive periods:

- Changes in equity between two consecutive periods = equity from the previous period to which the company's net profit has been added and from which the dividends distribution during that period has been deducted.

If there has been an increase in capital during the reporting period, it will be added to the share capital.

- Net cash position at the end of the period = cash from preceding period on balance sheet + net cash generated during the period stated in the cash-flow statement.

In each of the statements it is possible to find elements relative to:

- The financing strategy (equity, liabilities, repayments, financial expenses, dividends).

- The investment strategy (fixed assets, depreciation charges).

- The operating cycle (EBITDA, inventory, accounts receivable and payable).

5

Anna discovers the financial section of the business plan

Anna and Martin's new business « AM-Clean » will be a dedicated commercial cleaning company offering services that include cleaning of working spaces and public access areas, offices, industrial plants, commercial establishments and government facilities.

Martin and Anna have developed their business ideas for the project and have written their 5-year business plan.

This business plan consists of several sections, the main ones being:

- Mission, vision and values.
- Presentation of the product and/or services offer or a description of the business model.
- Market analysis – competitive environment.
- Objectives.
- Business strategy.
- Leadership team – management- human resources.
- Translation of the above elements into measurable data.

It is advisable to write a business plan for any business project as it allows the entrepreneur to ask a certain number of questions concerning all aspects of creating and developing a project and to find the appropriate answers.

The business plan is the compass that guides the founding leaders, who can refer to it within the first months of starting the company and adjust the objectives to the realities on a regular basis.

The financial section will then be reviewed over the following months and will be transformed into a projected monthly budget that will be compared to actual results.

This comprehensive document will enable Anna and Martin to present their project to potential investors, in the first place, certain ex-colleagues who are interested in the project and in second place to banking institutions and perhaps to local authorities as well.

After carrying out a detailed analysis of the market potential in their region and market prices for the services they wish to offer, Martin and Anna co-wrote sections 1 to 6 of the business plan which then enabled Martin to prepare the financial part while Anna carried on with her course on "finance for non-financials", specially designed to meet her needs and in keeping with the project.

Martin translated their objectives into financial elements in order to validate the feasibility of the project and in order to estimate the financing needs required.

After finishing her course, Anna studied the financial section of the business plan in order to understand the key elements and see if it is consistent with their strategy.

1. Projected income statement for 5 years:

The first document we are going to try and understand is the income statement. Naturally Martin gave Anna an additional sheet with the projected turnover detailed by customer, type of service offered and probability of transforming prospects into clients.

The projected income statement hereunder delivers an EBITDA at break-even from the second year onwards and Anna wonders if Martin's forecasting assumptions are not too optimistic.

Martin maintains that this EBITDA level is possible as the client who supports Martin and Anna's project has just agreed to sign a three-year contract due to a significant business increase in the area covered by "AM Clean".

5.1 Income Statment Forecast in EUR thousand

Years	1	2	3	4	5
Sales	252	653	810	1070	1457
Overheads	-70	-80	-110	-127	-152
Consummables (cleaning products)	-13	-26	-28	-32	-36
Wages	-199	-397	-458	-615	-835
Social Contributions	-67	-128	-150	-195	-263
Taxes	-5	-20	-24	-32	-44
EBITDA	-102	2	30	69	127
% of Sales	-40%	0%	4%	6%	9%
Depreciation	-8	-10	-13	-19	-23
Provisions and Amortization	0	0	0	0	0
EBIT	-110	-8	17	50	104
Financial Income or Expenses	-2	-2	-2	-3	-3
EBT	-112	-10	15	47	101
Corporate Tax					
Net Income	-112	-10	15	47	101
% of Sales	-44%	-2%	2%	4%	7%

Martin also explained that he took into account all the operating costs and that after having analyzed the workload schedule he factored in the hiring of six cleaners serving clients directly and one assistant who will help him with the employee scheduling and setting up a quality control system.

Martin informed Anna that in order to break even from the second year on and reach a positive net profit in year 3, he had to reduce their monthly gross income from €2 500 to €2 000 for the first three years and then to €2 250 in year 4.

The annual salary they had planned on to cover their respective household expenses will not be possible before year 5; therefore they will have to make personal sacrifices to manage their households.

He also explained to Anna that he withheld an average of 30 % in payroll taxes (social security contributions) from the employees' gross pay.

This rate could increase by 3 percentage points if regulations concerning social contributions for low salaries were to be modified once again plus it can increase (fluctuate upwards) when certain workforce thresholds are reached (10, 20 then 50 employees).

As an example, for this company, a one percentage point increase in contribution rates represents €2 000 in year 1, and increases to €8 000 in year 5, i.e. 0.5% of the sales.

Given these assumptions, the EBITDA to sales ratio will reach 9% in year 5.

During her course, Anna analyzed some competitors and noticed that the EBITDA to sales ratio came up at 8% and that the annual sales per total employee ratio for the most profitable companies was more than €38 000 per employee.

Therefore the annual sales per cleaner (operating employee) should be higher than this figure in order to cover at least salaries and expenses corresponding to employees and management.

She considers that by keeping Martin's salary and hers at almost the same level as those of the agents and assistant and also by keeping overhead costs and direct costs, such as cleaning products and tools, under strict control, a 9% EBITDA ratio is an ambitious yet realistic target.

Regarding corporate taxes, Martin has used the fiscal possibility of losses to be carried forward (i.e. previous losses deducted from actual profits).

However he has missed an amount of euros 13 000 in year 5, based on a average corporate tax rate of 30 %.

Martin will have to adjust the business plan accordingly.

For the time being, the income statement is accepted as presented. Now we have to move on to the cash-flow components in order to understand the cash-flow statement.

2. The cash-flow statement

In order to establish the cash-flow statement we will start by calculating the cash flow from operating activities, which will require adding:

- EBITDA from the income statement, i.e. earnings generated by the activity;
- The changes in working capital requirements (working capital variance) which allows for adjustments of the EBITDA due to payment timing differences concerning clients, suppliers, social charges (social security contributions).

Working capital needs represents the difference between current assets and current liabilities. It is the minimum amount required to cover its operating activities.

During the first year it is necessary to finance the working capital requirements entirely, then the following years, positive variances will require to be financed and negative variances will generate cash.

In the table below, a positive working capital is analyzed as an amount that requires funding.

5.2 Working Capital Forecast in EUR thousand

Years	1	2	3	4	5
Current Assets at Closing Date					
Cleaning Products Iventory					
Trade Receivables	38	98	122	160	219
Other Receivables (Sales Tax)	1	1	2	2	3
Total Assets	39	99	123	163	221
Trade Payables	7	8	11	13	15
Fiscal Liabilities (Sales Tax and Other Taxes)	6	16	20	27	36
Social Taxes Payables	22	43	50	65	88
Total Liabilities	35	67	81	105	139
Working Capital	4	32	42	58	82
Variance	4	28	10	16	24

Positive net change (a change in working capital that increases) between two years corresponds to a need in capital and a negative change (a change in working capital that decreases) corresponds to a cash generation.

The projected working capital requirements for « AM-Clean » were based on the following assumptions:

- No cleaning products will be kept in stock, as they will be considered as consumables.

- Agreed payment terms for clients will be 30 days upon receipt of invoice. As a precautionary measure Martin estimated (trade) accounts receivable at 45 days sales to which he adds the VAT charged to the client for his estimate.

- VAT paid on a monthly basis is the result of VAT billed on sales minus the deductible VAT paid on vendor invoices.

- Vendors are paid 30 days net in 80% of the cases, the remaining 20% are paid cash or within 30 days. « AM-Clean » is a young company so it will be difficult to negotiate payment terms with certain suppliers as long as the volume of business has not reached a significant size.

- Social security contributions are paid quarterly.

In general, the business plan should also be presented with a monthly cash flow forecast listing receipts and expenditures that will help to fine-tune short-term cash requirements.

The calculation of cash flow based on deducting all expenditures from all receipts is called cash flow calculations using direct methodology. This methodology can be used on a daily basis or to establish the monthly cash flow forecast.

In fact cash flow requirements can vary considerably from one month to another for companies that are heavily dependent on seasonality.

Given the company's projected expansion, « AM-Clean » estimates of the annual working capital requirements reflect continued growth (from €4 000 to €82 000) that will need to be financed.

5.3 Cash Flow Statement Forecast in EUR thousand

Years	1	2	3	4	5
EBITDA	-102	2	30	69	127
Financial Income or Expenses	-2	-2	-2	-3	-3
Corporate Tax					
Working Capital Variance	-4	-28	-10	-16	-24
Cash Flow from Opearing Activities	-107	-29	18	50	100
Purchase of Non Current Assets	-40	-10	-15	-30	-20
Proceeds from Sale of Non Current Assets					
Cash Flow from Investing Activities	-40	-10	-15	-30	-20
Capital Increase (or Decrease)	50				
Dividends Paid					
Long Term Borrowings	40				
Shareholders Account	70	30			
Shareholders Account (Salaries not Paid)					
Debts Repayements		-8	-8	-8	-8
Cash Flow from Financing Activities	160	22	-8	-8	-8
Increase or Decrease in Net Cash	13	-17	-5	12	72

Once she had understood and validated the working capital assumptions, Anna moved on to examine the cash-flow statement.

Based on the above assumptions and the projected income statement, it appears that in year 1 and year 2, the « AM-Clean » operating activity will consume (use or burn) cash: €107 000 in year 1 and €29 000 in year 2. Starting from year 3 the activity will generate cash.

After determining net cash flow from operating activities, Martin estimated the amount of office and cleaning equipment required at €40 000. He scoped the equipment needs for the first two years. Subsequent needs were estimated according to the projected revenue per client.

If the investments cannot be financed with cash generated by the activity, alternative funding such as capital contribution from shareholders or a loan will have to be found.

Total funding requirements amount to €160 000.

Martin and Anna plan to invest a maximum of €120 000 in their project. They will invest practically all of their savings. They will provide €50 000 in capital and €70 000 in cash booked as shareholders debts that will not earn interest. In order to reach the €70 000, Anna and Martin also obtained €10 000 in funds from a national scheme that helps the unemployed set up a business.

They are going to negotiate a loan of €40 000 to finance their investments in equipment.

Anna can use her personal borrowing capacity against her personal assets but for the moment Martin recommends that she does not use her estate as a personal guarantee to obtain a loan.

He is confident that they will obtain financing from a banking institution and/or from a government related credit institution as their business plan is solid and they plan to employ seven people from day one.

The cash flow forecast will show a negative closing balance in year 2 and 3: Martin and Anna will have to apply for an overdraft of €30 000 in addition to the loan of €40 000.

In order to calculate the overdraft amount, Martin drew up a monthly cash flow forecast (receipts and expenditures table).The monthly cash flow can vary due to sales seasonality and a safety margin should be calculated in case of a late payment from a client, (margin adjustment to cover late payments) even if it is only by a few days.

A late payment from a client can spark a cash crisis and may require urgent negotiations with the company's bank if the cash flow situation is tight, especially in the early stages of a business.

Many companies underestimate their cash-flow needs during the start-up period. As financial issues may arise as soon as the end of the first year, this could undermine the credibility of management in its ability to make credible forecasts and make it difficult or even impossible to obtain additional financing. Under these circumstances, only the shareholders are able to supplement the company's financial resources.

Martin and Anna know that like many other companies they could be faced with the possibility of not being paid and having to defer all or part of their wages; a partners' current account will be entered as a liability on the balance sheet to show company debts to the shareholders.

Anna, Martin and their respective spouses are aware that they will have to make lifestyle changes and financial sacrifices in order to develop the company. The spouses who are both employees in local companies will have to cover all the basic family expenses.

3. The balance sheet

Martin created a projected balance sheet for the first five years and used the following elements:

- On the assets side:

- He recorded the forecasted investments minus the accumulated depreciation: we can therefore see that at the end of the financial period, the net amount invested by the company in office and cleaning equipment is €40 000 less the depreciation value spread over five years, i.e. €8 000 per year. He used the same straight line depreciation method for subsequent investments.

- He then incorporated the receivables estimated in the working capital calculations at the close of the financial year.

- Cash availability was recorded as a negative net asset which made Anna realize that the closing cash balance for years 2 and 3 will be negative and a solution will have to be found: they will have to apply for a bank overdraft, or defer management's salaries or ask certain clients for a down payment or provide additional share capital.

It sometimes happens that management is obliged to combine all of these options. Of course, deferring management's salaries is only acceptable for a limited amount of time and if the financial management is sound.

- Net equity:

- Capital provided by the shareholders (investors) and the company's net result of the year and retained profit or losses are reported under net equity subtotal.

Given the losses for years 1 and 2, the company's net equity will be negative. Legally it cannot be less than half of the share capital.

Martin explains to Anna that according to company laws in France, equity capital has to be restored to at least half of the company's net equity capital within a period of two years following the reporting year, which in our case would be €25 000 at the end of year 3 at the latest.

– In the case of « AM-Clean », it will have to address the need to increase capital by incorporating the €70 000 shareholders debt account.

– This means that the current account will be incorporated directly into the shareholders' equity when the time comes and that it may be at risk of not being repaid to shareholders.

– Shareholders who invested in total €120 000 in the company have a right to expect returns which are called dividends as soon as the company makes a profit and shows a positive cash flow position, which will take at least 5 years.

– Retained earnings include the accumulated sum of the net income or net loss from previous financial periods.

• Liabilities

– Long-term debts correspond to the loan that Anna intends to ask the banks in order to finance their investments. This loan will be reduced each year with repayments, excluding financial costs that can be found on the income statement, just after EBITDA.

– At this stage Martin has not made any risk provisions in the case of litigations.

– Short-term debts are made up of accounts payable and accrued taxes and social security liabilities calculated for working capital requirements.

– Martin should have shown the bank overdrafts on the liabilities side instead he presented them on the assets side as cash equivalents with a minus sign. He did so to facilitate Anna's understanding of the business plan. The overdrafts represent what the company owes to the bank or will need to require as o

5.4 **Balance Sheet Forecast in EUR thousand**

Years	1	2	3	4	5
Non Current Assets	32	32	34	45	42
Inventory					
Trade Receivables	38	98	122	160	219
Other Receivables	1	1	2	2	3
Cash and Cash Equivalent	13	-4	-9	2	74
Total Assets	83	127	148	210	338
Share Capital	50	50	50	50	50
Reserves					
Retained Earnings		-112	-122	-107	-61
Profit or Loss of the year	-112	-10	15	47	101
Net Equity	*-62*	*-72*	*-57*	*-11*	*91*
Financial Debts (long term)	40	32	24	16	8
Shareholders Account	70	100	100	100	100
Trade Payables	7	8	11	13	15
Fiscal Liabilities	6	16	20	27	36
Social Contributions and Leave Accruals	22	43	50	65	88
Total Liabilities	83	127	148	210	338

Anna would like to be sure that the financial data in the business plan are correctly reported and calculated.

Martin explains that cash flow is one of the key indicators to track performance and ensure consistency in reporting results. He suggests using the balance sheet and cash flow statement to perform a consistency check.

**Cash Flow Forecast Calculations
Control between 2 Periods**

Years	1	2	3	4	5
Cash at the Start of the Period	0	13	-4	-9	2
Increase or Decreae in Net Cash	13	-17	-5	12	72
Cash at the End of the Period	13	-4	-9	2	74

6

Draft of the key performance indicators (KPI) dashboard

Martin provides Anna with a monthly KPI dashboard, which is an activity report that monitors performance and helps to identify the strengths and weaknesses of the company.

Producing a dashboard presupposes that company accounts are updated regularly in accordance with accounting principles and issued on a monthly basis, a few days after the month end. Performance can then be analyzed and compared to the forecast or to the budget and if necessary corrective measures will then be implemented as soon as possible.

Certain decisions even if they are taken rapidly, may require some time to implement, given the delays needed to negotiate bank overdrafts, collection and payment periods or legal deadlines (statutory time limits) related to work schedule changes such as working hours, recruitment or downsizing.

The dashboard created by Martin includes the following elements:

1. Operations

- Personnel: number by function and variance.
- Revenue generated per person and its progress.
- Total salary costs and average per employee.
- Average gross salary of operational staff and management

2. Performance

- Weight of operating costs to sales.
- EBITDA return to sales.

3. Cash-flow

- Clients' average payment terms.
- Total cash available or amount of overdraft used.

6.1 Key Performance Indicators Dashboard

Years	1	2	3	4	5
Managers	2	2	2	2	2
Support Functions	1	1	1	2	3
Operational Staff (Cleaners)	6	15	18	23	31
Total Employees	9	18	21	27	36
Sales	252000	652500	810000	1069500	1457000
Personnel Costs	266160	525312	617376	810300	1097760
Average Employee Cost	29573	29184	29399	30011	30493
Sales / Total Employees	28000	36250	38571	39611	40472
Sales / Operational Staff	42000	43500	45000	46500	47000
Cleaning Products / Sales	5%	4%	4%	3%	3%
Overheads / Sales	28%	12%	14%	12%	10%
Salaries / Sales	79%	61%	58%	58%	57%
Charges sociales / Sales	27%	20%	19%	18%	18%
Impôts et taxes / Sales	2%	3%	3%	3%	3%
EBITDA / Sales	-40%	0%	4%	6%	9%
Customers average payement terms in days	45d	45d	45d	45d	45d
Closing Cash Position	13	-4	-9	2	74
Manager Monthly Gross Salary	2000	2000	2000	2250	2500
Avg. Operational Staff Monthly Gross Salary	1800	1820	1840	1870	1900

Anna wonders if she doesn't need a more detailed monthly dashboard in order to monitor the company's performance more closely.

Anna would also like to use the dashboard at the quarterly staff meetings she plans to organize.

She suggests that Martin add more information such as:

- Productivity ratio.

- Number of downtime hours.

- Number of clients gained or lost with an estimate of the respective turnovers.

- The cash position.

Analysis of the man-hour productivity requires having a more detailed management control that will provide valuable indicators concerning operational staff productivity and pricing coherence.

As a result Martin proposes to include the total number of hours paid during the reporting period (weekly, monthly etc.) and the number of hours actually worked and billed.

In fact, if for 100 hours paid, only 70 % are actually productive i.e. used to carry out cleaning services and therefore billed then « AM-Clean » will not be profitable unless it raises its prices to a level that will no longer be competitive.

7

Anna and Martin create their company « AM-Clean»

Anna and Martin are motivated and convinced that their project is viable. They presented it to their potential client who was very enthusiastic about the quality of the project and the services offered.

Anna and Martin have chosen the legal structure of their business, it will be a limited company (in UK or a corporation in USA) responsible in its own right for everything it does and its finances are separate to their personal finances. Any profit it makes is owned by the company, after it pays corporate tax. The company can then share its profits.

The decision to create « AM-Clean » has been made, with a share capital of €50 000 broken down as follows:

- Anna will provide €20 000 and will hold 40 % of the company's shares.

- Martin will provide €15 000 and therefore hold 30 % of the shares.

  Three other friends will provide the remaining €15 000 which represents 30 % of the capital. They will not be involved in the management of the company but hope that the €5 000 invested by each of them will contribute to its development.

  They also hope that « AM-Clean » will grow in the years to come and that dividends will be paid in a few years' time. However, they are well aware of the risk they have taken: in fact if the company does not succeed they will have lost their investment (like any shareholder would!).

The business plan has set forth the need for a total funding of €160 000 of which Anna and Martin will provide an additional €70 000 as a shareholders debt account earning no interest, in order to strengthen their borrowing capacity in the eyes of the banks.

In order to finalize the global financing plan, they need to borrow €40 000 to purchase cleaning and office equipment. They will also apply for an overdraft facility amounting to €30 000 in order to manage delays in client payments. This overdraft corresponds to the maximum negative cash balance obtained when the monthly cash flow forecast was drawn up.

Martin and Anna met with three banks to present their « AM-Clean » project. After several meetings and requests for additional information, only one regional bank agreed to finance their investments.

Support from local government authorities who proposed office space at a reduced rental fee for three years and a 60 % guarantee on the loan from governmental credit institutions dedicated to SMEs helped convince the regional bank to help « AM-Clean ».

The regional bank agreed to discuss the possibility of obtaining an overdraft (or a similar product) after six months of business.

Local government authorities supported the project due to its potential for creating jobs: seven within the first year!

Drawing up the company's articles of incorporation, depositing the funds and registering the company took less than 15 days.

Anna was pleasantly surprised, due to the prevailing misconception that starting a company in France is a lengthy and cumbersome process.

The company is created three months before year 1 in order to set up the hiring process and start searching for clients. The year 1 statements will include costs incurred in the last quarter of the previous year, so it will be a 15-month business year, which is exceptionally allowed for the first financial year.

Anna and Martin move into their office and start carrying out various administrative duties:

- They need to register with the tax authorities, notably to select a scheme for VAT returns. Due to its legal structure « AM-Clean » is subject to corporate tax.

- They also need to register the company with the different organizations and social security systems and choose the social coverage (pension scheme) in accordance with the provisions of the collective agreement for the cleaning industry to which « AM-Clean » will belong to.

- They call on an IT services company to create their website, purchase equipment and set up the computer network.

- Anna finalizes the first contract with the client who has supported them since the beginning of the project and accepts his requests namely concerning cleaning schedules and concludes that they will need to hire three people. They plan to hire another three when they sign the next contracts.

Martin begins the hiring process and does not encounter too many difficulties in finding staff but wastes a lot of time finalizing employment contracts, as there are a number of different types of contracts available. He also discovers the complexity of the timetable planning for the agents (cleaning staff).

He has to constantly juggle between the number of hours needed to do the job: the staff's schedule needs relating to their personal lives and the legal constraints such as:

- Minimum number of hours required for a permanent part-time contract.

- Restrictions related to shift work (number of assignments with an unpaid break per agent per day).

- Quotas for overtime, night shifts etc.

The company will be open for business from 02 January in year 1 and the first 15 days will be used for training the operational staff.

8

Business development
and financial results of « AM-Clean »
after three financial years

At the end of the third year, Anna and Martin have mixed feelings concerning the financial results of « AM-Clean ».

Compared to the forecasted results in the business plan, the achievements are on the whole below expectations. Even though sales figures over a period of three years are higher than the forecast, all the other indicators are rather disappointing (EBITDA, cash-flow etc.)

However, if they analyze the way their various achievements have progressed, they have every reason to be happy with the company's expansion. Sales have increased significantly year after year: EBITDA ratio is improving as is the cash-flow generated by the activity.

Anna and Martin have to present the company's results to the shareholders who expect answers concerning its development as well as deviations from the business plan.

They are glad to make this first presentation to the shareholders, who are also their friends because they will have to repeat the exercise when they go and see their bank to ask for additional financing, required to meet the needs of new clients.

In view of these meetings, they have prepared their financial documents: income statement, cash-flow statement and the balance sheet for the last three years. (Annex II) but to make it easier to understand, they have also prepared a document that groups all the key performance indicators (KPIs) that they are going to go over.

1. Revenue and pricing

Sales progressed over the three years, the targeted clients did indeed sign service contracts with « AMClean » but the expected profitability of a 4 % EBITDA margin (return on sales ratio) was not reached: the company did not create value as expected. The main reasons are:

- Instead of increasing in years 2 and 3, sales divided by the number of working staff decreased by 6.25%, from €42 500 to €40 000: and it was necessary to hire additional staff to cover all services hours requested by customers.

- Hourly staff rates increased by 1 %.

- Hourly rates for productive hours increased more rapidly than sales revenue turnover as a certain number of employees waited for more than two hours between assignments.

- Anna and Martin had failed to gauge the impact of these work interruptions (downtime) when they calculated the cost of service and established the price proposals for their clients. The shifts (i.e. the number of work interruptions possible in one day) that are legally authorized are not sufficient to adapt the working schedules of staff to the clients' needs.

- Also, they had not measured the impact of non-productive hours between the two previous financial periods because sales revenue per person had increased between years 1 and 2.

- The number of agents at the end of year 3 was 21 instead of the 18 forecasted.

2. Company operating costs

- Owing to the complexity of labor laws concerning the choice of contracts available for each hiring situation and the number of rules and regulations that need to be complied with when planning work schedules, Martin and Anna decided to employ a human resources manager.

This HR manager has also dealt with provisions related to threshold changes.

« AM-Clean » had a staff of 9 at the end of year 1 and went up to 16 at the end of year 2 and then 25 at the end of year 3 meaning that over the last three years they have had to deal with two workforce threshold changes, moving up to 10 employees and then 20.

- Social security contributions amounted to 31 % of the staff's gross salaries instead of the 30 % forecasted in the Business Plan due to a threshold change.

In order to limit the impact of the increase on the company's expenses,

8.1 Operating KPIs Forecast vs. Actual

Years	1		2		3	
	F	A	F	A	F	A
Operationnal Staff	6	6	15	12	18	21
Sales	252	240	653	510	810	840
Customers Average Payment Terms in days	45d	45d	45d	48d	45d	54d
Sales / Operationnal Staff	42000	40000	43500	42500	45000	40000
EBITDA	-102	-91	2	-41	30	-8
Salaries / Sales	106%	103%	81%	88%	76%	84%
Cleaning Products / Sales	5%	4%	4%	3%	4%	3%
Overheads / Sales	28%	29%	12%	15%	14%	11%
EBITDA / Sales	-40%	-38%	0%	-8%	4%	-1%

8.2 Salaries KPIs Forecast vs. Actual

Years	1		2		3	
	F	A	F	A	F	A
Manager Monthly Gross Salary	2000	1500	2000	1500	2000	1500
Avg. Operating Staff Monthly Gross Salary	1800	1775	1820	1793	1840	1811

Anna and Martin reduced their gross annual salary to €1 500 over three years instead of the forecasted amount of €2 000. They will maintain the same gross salary for years 4 and 5.

3. Decline in cash flow

Causes of the decline:

- Increases in staff costs had a direct impact on cash flow.
- Clients who usually paid within 48 days in year 2, averaged 54 days in year 3.

In order to limit the adverse effects, Martin took the following measures:

- Reduced the impact of the longer payment periods (accounts receivable collection period) on the working capital requirements: Martin negotiated a down payment on services invoiced with two major clients; he informed them that more than 75 % of his costs concerned salaries payable at the end of each month and as compensation for the longer payment terms he needed an advance (down payment) from them.

- Limited the impact of the longer client payment terms on the cash-flow positions: Martin extended the suppliers' terms of payment but Anna disagreed with this solution, as she believes that suppliers should not be burdened with their cash-flow problems.

- Limited the decline in the cash-flow situation and given the approved maximum overdraft of €30 000 facility: Martin and Anna deferred their salary payments to a later date and reported it as shareholders current liabilities.

4. Medium-term financing needs

Due to the sales growth of « AM-Clean » which will increase by 32 % in year 4, they will have to invest in €40 000 worth of cleaning equipment and will have to apply for a new bank loan.

In light of this, Martin and Anna will update their business plan for the following three years (years 4/5/6) and provide proof that their company can pay the additional annuities.

« AM-Clean » has paid the installments of the first loan of €8 000 per year and if they obtain this additional loan the company will have to repay another €8 000. Cash outflow for financing will therefore amount to €16 000 per year.

Seeking financing is a real challenge for business leaders and it is one of the most stressful and frustrating periods because:

- on the one hand management has proven that their project is viable with a quality portfolio of clients, an increase in sales and good management practices;

- but, on the other hand, given the losses for the 3 financial periods and the increase in working capital requirements, the banks refuse to finance them and propose instead to raise the capital or open it up to new investors.

Anna and Martin have made enquiries about the possibility of opening the capital to new investors but they are aware that this option is a long drawn-out process and they are not prepared to deal with this eventuality.

Furthermore, they have exhausted all the possibilities to provide additional cash and risk having to defer a part of their salaries once more. In order to start restoring the shareholders' equity which is currently negative, Anna and Martin have incorporated their current accounts into share capital and increased the capital by €70 000.

It is very difficult to convince a credit institution to provide financing, especially during the first three years of a company and it is also very hard to meet the requirements of any funding schemes.

Banks are not in the habit of making the distinction between a young company (less than 3 years) that loses money but is showing potential growth with an order book and a company with structural problems.

Both companies show indicators like EBITDA, net income, net cash flow generated and equity capital in the red. It is difficult to convince a bank to provide funding based only on growth in sales and client portfolio. It sometimes works for internet business related companies!

The revised business plan, order book and measures taken to improve productivity promise a balanced budget for « AM-Clean » from year 4 but how can they convince any banks or any government supported credit institutions dedicated to business?

Fortunately local government authorities, concerned by the employment situation in the region helped convince the Banque Publique d'Investissement (BPI) to guarantee 70 % of the additional financing so that the bank would accept to finance their investments.

Now that « AM-Clean » has finally obtained its loan: it can continue its development and take corrective actions to achieve its profitability goal.

8.3 Cash Flow KPIs Forecast vs. Actual

Years	1		2		3	
	F	A	F	A	F	A
Cash Flow from Operating Activities	-107	-102	-29	-44	18	-18
Cash Flow fron Investing Activities	-40	-40	-10	-7	-15	-7
Cash Flow from Financing Activities	160	160	22	21	-8	7
Net Cash Flow	13	18	-17	-30	-5	-19
Cash at the End of the Period	13	18	-4	-13	-9	-31

8.4 Net Equity Forecast vs. Actual

Years	1		2		3	
	F	A	F	A	F	A
Net Income	-112	-101	-10	-52	15	-21
Net Equity	-62	-51	-72	-103	-57	-54

9

Required adjustments and economic setbacks over the next two years

Anna and Martin have understood the issues concerning the adequacy of working hours and the clients' needs. As a result they know they have to increase the global volume of productive hours.

Therefore during the last quarter of year 3 they have automated their employee planning which includes a clock in/out on site application and a service costing tool that helps to forecast prices using customer needs and actual costs.

The objective is to look for profitable growth.

By testing this tool on existing contracts, they realized that prices charged for previous jobs did not take into account employees' non-productive time correctly, between two cleaning assignments.

This issue could be solved in various ways:

- The scheduling tool that analyses the workload schedule of each employee according to the time periods requested by the clients proposes an optimized reallocation of resources with a change in work location for certain employees while taking into account their availabilities.

- This tool can also include non-productive time between two assignments that will be factored into the prices proposed to clients.

- Constraints related to employees' legal work hours could do with more flexibility but this is not a decision the company can take on its own.

It depends on comprehensive negotiations at national level.

An industry-wide agreement has recently been signed in France concerning the clarification of work hours, number of shifts, etc. but there is certainly room for more improvement.

A staff representative for « AM-Clean » employees has called for a pay increase on their behalf as salaries remained stable in the last three years. Employees also consider that their salaries do not reflect the increase in sales over the last three years and they feel that the automated employee scheduling is a form of monitoring that is seen as a sign of distrust on the part of management.

Anna and Martin decide to have a staff meeting to show them the company's key performance indicators that they have prepared for the shareholders.

They also take the time to explain why it is important for the company to set up an automated time and attendance system (clock in/out system).

In fact this software tool will facilitate future work scheduling, generate pay-roll slips and enable charge-out rate calculations based on real-time effective working hours.

Anna and Martin inform the staff that not only have they decided to reduce their own salaries but they have also deferred them in order to comply with the bank overdraft approval conditions.

After explaining the company's situation, Anna proposes setting up an incentive program for non-managerial staff.

The employees suggest that they form 2 working groups that will be in charge of proposing the indicators and establishing measuring standards that will determine the incentive payments:

- the first group will include Martin and staff who will be in charge of thinking about the operational performance indicators;
- the other group will consist of Anna, some of the agents, the quality control assistant and two clients (including the first client). They will be in charge of working on the quality expectations of clients.

Each group will present its findings after having held three meetings.

Two months later, the two groups share and discuss their proposals, sometimes quite passionately but always in the interest of the company. They finalize the agreement that they will present at a general staff meeting.

The agreement is based on three categories of criteria:

• Quality indicators:

– punctuality on-site at client's premises;

– absenteeism rate;

– customer satisfaction rate obtained by means of a detailed questionnaire drawn up by the executive assistant who trained in service quality evaluation methods.

Discussions with clients indicate that they are quite receptive to the use of green cleaning products (biodegradable and less harmful) so a minimum percentage of environmentally friendly products will form part of those used by « AM-Clean ».

• Operational performance indicators:

– average sales volume per cleaner;

– percentage of cleaning products used in proportion of sales;

– EBITDA to sales ratio.

• Cash generation indicator:

– days sales outstanding (DSO)

However, Martin realized that it was actually possible to reach one of the objectives (client satisfaction, punctuality, absenteeism rate) that produce an incentive payment, without taking into account the overall health of the company.

He therefore insisted on adding two conditional clauses to the agreement: the company must show a net profit and a positive net cash position in order to trigger an incentive payment.
Once the employees had understood the real motivations behind the introduction of an automated work scheduling and time and attendance system they accepted and signed the agreement.

The agreement provides for a total incentive payout that represents a maximum of 3 % of the total payroll of agents and support staff.

A cost controller was hired in order to follow up the work-scheduling system and to calculate price offers for clients. He will also assist Martin in his duties.

Other events have also disrupted the company's pace of development:

• A competitor has moved into the region and has taken away one of the clients who represented 10 % of « AM-Clean's » sales. Anna was in the middle of renegotiating the contract as this was one of the clients whose price offer had been under estimated. « AM-Clean » maintained the new adjusted price proposal and lost its client to the competitor.

• Due to the ongoing economic crisis and in particular at the end of year 4, 60 % of « AM-Clean's » long-standing clients reduced the volume of services purchased on an hourly basis for year 5.

To meet these new challenges:

• Anna decided to use the staff incentive scheme as a competitive edge that made clients receptive to the company's social responsibility and its spirit of sustainability.

• Anna hired a sales manager in January of year 5 to assist her in looking for new business opportunities in an extended area, which helped compensate for various losses and continued to develop the company.

It should be noted that sales increased by 32 % in year 4 compared to year 3 and grew by 40 % in year 5 compared to year 4.

Thanks to the automated work-scheduling system and the new pricing calculations, AM-Clean is on its way to achieving profitable growth. Thus the operating margin rate (EBITDA performance ratio) progressed from €40 000 in year 3 to €44 500.

Anna and Martin maintained their monthly gross salaries at the same level as previous years i.e. €1 500.

In light of all the measures that were taken and thanks to the efforts made by all the stakeholders, Anna and Martin, reassured by their new financial forecasts, are confident in their ability to continue to develop their company.

10

Success as well as new challenges

With sales amounting to 1.56 million euros in year 5, AM-Clean reached an operating margin of 7 % (EBITDA to sales ratio) that is €114 000 and a net profit of 6 % (return on sales) of €87 000

10.1 «AM-Clean» performance in EUR thousand

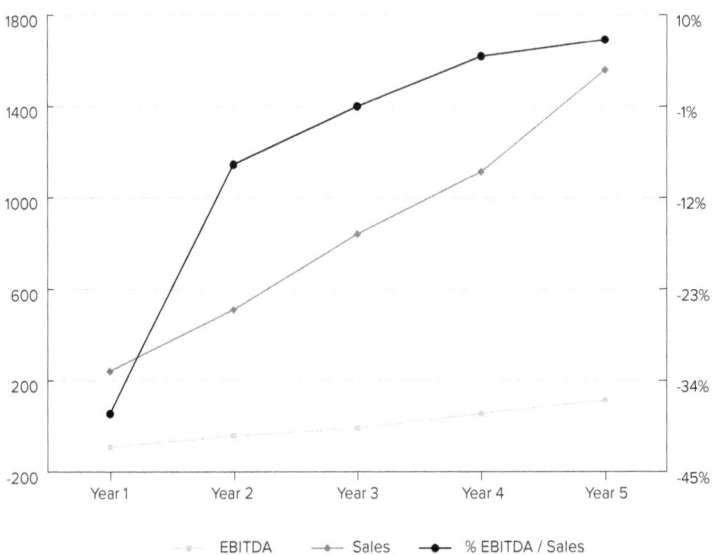

Even though AM-Clean was profitable in years 4 and 5 it is still not subject to corporate tax based on current tax regulations that allow previous losses to be carried forward.

Accumulated losses for the last 3 financial years amount to €174 000 and the accumulated profits at the end of year 5 are €119 000.

Losses amounting to €55 000 remain to be carried forward.

10.2 «AM-Clean» Net Cash Flow Generated or Used in EUR thousand

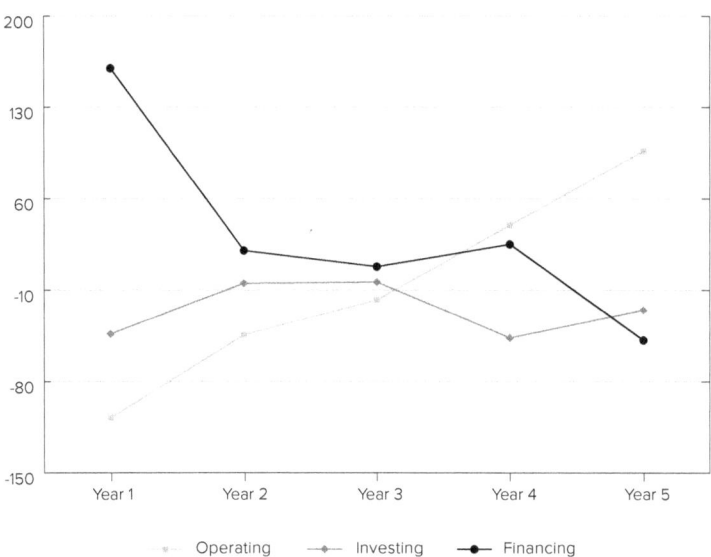

The activity generated €95 000 of cash flow from operations which enabled the company to continue investing in better cleaning equipment and above all, pay Anna and Martin's salaries from year 2.

10.3 «AM-Clean» Net Cash Flow and Net Cash Position in EUR thousand

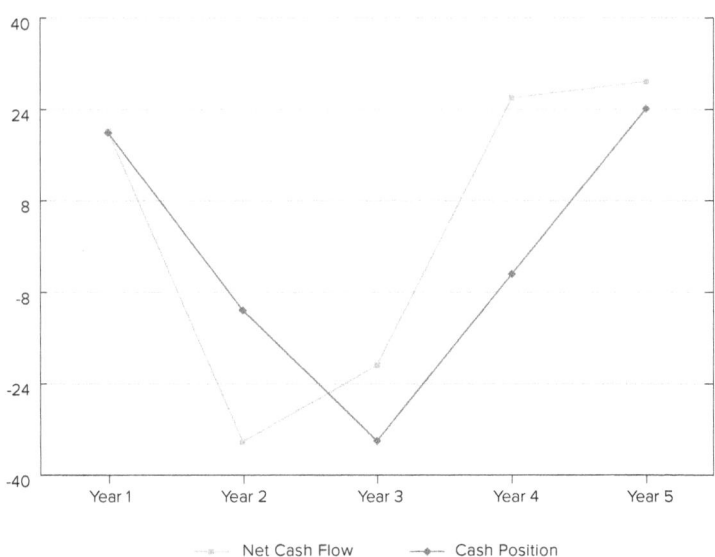

The €29 000 of net cash generated during year 5 also meant total cash available amounted €24 000 at the end of period 5.

10.4 «AM-Clean» Net Equity in EUR thousand

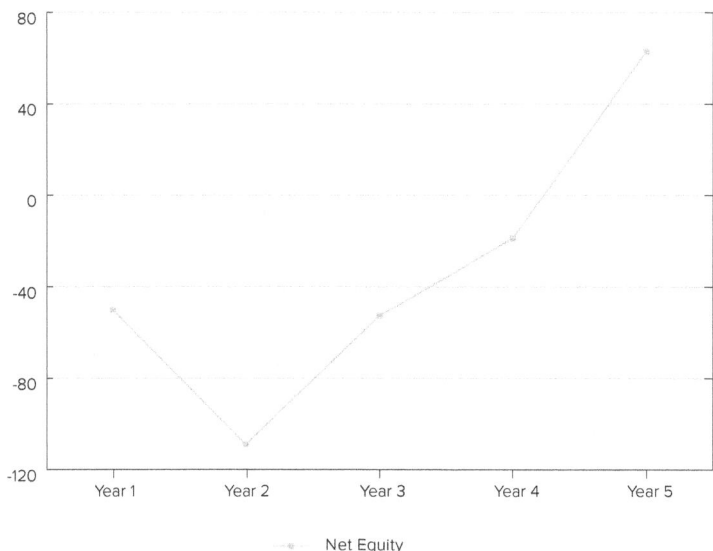

Net Equity

A net income of €87 000 also enabled AM-Clean to restore its level of net equity which was still negative at €22 000 end of year 4. With the addition of the net income from period 5, the amount of net equity went up to €65 000 and therefore represents more than 50 % of the share capital.

During year 6, AM-Clean will have to foresee cash outflows related to the payment of Anna and Martin's wages dating back to year 3. They had also been deferred due to a shortage of cash.

The incentive agreement signed at the beginning of year 4 will take effect in year 6 and is estimated at €13 000 i.e. 1 % of the gross payroll costs. This amount will be shared among the employees but excludes the director-shareholders.

It should be noted that this incentive payment even if it is limited as per the total payroll, represents 10 % of the earnings before tax.

AM-Clean will also have to provide for payment of the corporate tax as there will be no more previous losses to carry forward, so it will be subject to 15 % tax limited to €38 120 of earnings and 33.33 % over that on its earnings before tax (EBT).

Based on a €130 000 EBT and a remaining €55 000 of losses to be carried forward, the tax amount is estimated at a maximum of €20 000

And finally it should be noted that Anna and Martin have not provided for dividend payments before year 7. They have however planned on increasing their monthly gross salary to €2 500 per month as from year 6.

Anna and Martin wonder if they should continue their development as the economic crisis is not yet over and numerous businesses in their region are going through a difficult period.

They have several questions in mind:

- They would like to expand their business to an adjacent region... but should they exceed the 49-employee threshold in this period of crisis?

- The HR manager calculated the global cost of this implementation at 3 % of sales (additional contributions, time to implement and deal with the additional administrative requirements).The extra costs could possibly be offset by the CICE (Competitiveness and Employment tax credit) a tax incentive scheme that was introduced recently but Anna and Martin have some doubts concerning the stability of tax laws and social legislation.

- They would also like to diversify their «green » services offer and propose it to nursing homes and clinics: these are new skills that they need to develop and it also entails applying new scheduling methods.

To finance this diversification, Anna and Martin will have to look for new investors which mean:

- Creating a business plan that integrates these new opportunities and carrying out a business valuation.

- Building a new governance plan and preparing for the possibility that they may no longer be their company's majority shareholders.

Anna and Martin will take the time to think it over during year 6. This will also be the year they will need to learn analytical and financial skills in order to make a full assessment of their company and evaluate their business performance.

This way they will be able to defend their own interests and those of the business when dealing with new potential investors, who will not hesitate to impose new management rules and objectives...

But for the moment let them enjoy their success!

Despite all the sacrifices and frustration, Anna and Martin are happy that they decided to embark on a business venture. The list of reasons that led them to start a business is still valid. They have become more independent, created 39 new jobs and foresee an improvement in the company's financial situation as well as theirs.

Conclusion

When the media spotlight focuses on a certain number of business leaders, whose only objectives are to increase their earnings or on shareholders whose only interest is to increase their ROI, to the detriment of long-term vision, it simply draws attention to a limited number of large multinational corporations!

A company is a global system that includes management, shareholders, employees, clients and all other stakeholders, who in the majority of cases work towards a common goal: attain long-term success for their business.

Therefore, it is important to keep in mind that SMEs contribute significantly to job creation:

- In France SMEs created 600 000 jobs between 2002 and 2012.

- 85% of net new jobs in the EU between 2002 and 2010 were created by small and medium sized enterprises (SMEs).

- In the USA , SMEs accounted for 63 percent of the net new jobs created between 1993 and mid-2013 (or 14.3 million of the 22.9 million net new jobs).

Despite the importance of SMEs for job creation and production, most of the SME firms face higher barriers to external financing than large firms, which limit their growth and development.
The business background of « AM-Clean » is similar to so many other companies around the world who are eager to develop their businesses if only:

- Public authorities would realize that there is a need for more in-depth analysis concerning the impact of their economic, fiscal and social policies on the development of SMEs. Political leaders have a tendency to define their economic policies in terms of major corporations that use rampant lobbying to push decisions in their favor. This generally leads public authorities to pass laws that are inconsistent with the realities of SMEs and that are moreover, difficult to implement.

- The various credit institutions would accept to finance them during the first three years by adopting new rules for financing agreements that are more practical and in line with the company's potential, the quality of its management and the skills of its employees.

Want to follow on Anna and Matin's path to entrepreneurshitp? Start your business plan now!

Should you wish to become an investor, start a financial analysis of your targeted insvestment!

Appendices

Answers:
Test your business knowledge

1. A 5% increase in sales corresponds to an equivalent capacity to increase salaries.

– False

2. There are different margins level ratios in a business.

– True

3. A company's net income can be a profit or a loss.

– True

4. Profits earned by a company do not automatically result in an increase in cash flow.

– True

5. The difference between profit and cash generated by the company is only tied to dividend payments.

– False

6. Cash flow generated from the company's operating activities will help determine if the company has the means to invest and to comply with loan repayment terms.

– True

7. If company expenses increase by 3% and sales by 2% its income ratio will improve.

– False

8. EBITDA is the operational indicator of performance that is most frequently used. EBITDA gives the company leeway to invest or finance its business.

– True

9. If client payment terms are extended, the impact on cash flow will be negative.

– True

10. If supplier payment terms are extended, the impact on cash flow will be temporarily favorable.

– True

II

«AM-Clean»
Actual Numbers over 5 years

II.1 **Income Statment in EUR thousand**

Years	1	2	3	4	5
Sale	240	510	840	1113	1558
Overheads	-70	-75	-92	-121	-149
Consummables (cleaning poducts)	-10	-17	-27	-32	-45
Wages	-185	-337	-536	-650	-900
Social Contributions	-61	-111	-173	-215	-295
Taxes	-5	-11	-21	-39	-55
EBITDA	-91	-41	-8	55	114
% of Sales	-38%	-8%	-1%	5%	7%
Depreciation	-8	-9	-11	-19	-23
Provisions and Amortization	0	0	0	0	0
EBIT	-99	-50	-19	36	91
Financial Income or Expenses	-2	-2	-2	-3	-3
EBT	-101	-52	-21	32	87
Corporate Tax					
Net Income	-101	-52	-21	32	87
% of Sales	-42%	-10%	-2%	3%	6%

II.2 Working Capital in EUR thousand

Years	1	2	3	4	5
Current Assets at Closing Date					
Cleaning Products Inventory	5	10	7	7	7
Trade Receivables	36	82	151	195	249
Other Receivables (Sales Tax)	1	2	3	3	3
Total Assets	42	94	161	205	259
Customer Advances		20	40	55	60
Trade Payables	6	12	19	17	16
Fiscial Liabilities	6	14	25	32	42
Social Taxes Payables	20	37	58	72	98
Total Liabilities	33	83	142	176	215
Working Capital	9	11	19	28	44
Variance	9	1	8	9	15

II.3 Cash Flow Statement in EUR thousand

Years	1	2	3	4	5
EBITDA	-91	-41	-8	55	114
Financial Income or Expenses	-2	-2	-2	-4	-4
Corporate Tax					
Working Capital Variance	-9	-1	-8	-9	-15
Cash Flow from Operating Activities	-102	-44	-18	42	95
Purchase of Non Current Assets	-40	-7	-7	-40	-20
Proceeds from Sale orf Non Current Assets					
Cash Flow from Investing Activities	-40	-7	-7	-40	-20
Capital Increase (or Decrease)	50		70		
Dividends Paid					
Long Term Borrowings	40			40	
Shareholders Account	70		-70		
Shareholders Account (Salaries not Paid)		29	15		-29
Debts Repayments		-8	-8	-16	-16
Cash Flow from Financing Activities	160	21	7	24	-45
Increase or Decrease in Net Cash	18	-30	-19	26	-45

II.4 **Balance Sheet in EUR thousand**

Years	1	2	3	4	5
Non Current Assets	32	30	26	47	44
Inventory	5	10	7	7	7
Trade Receivables	36	82	151	195	249
Other Receivables	1	2	3	3	3
Cash and Cash Equivalent	18	0	0	0	24
Total Assets	92	123	187	252	327
Share Capital	50	50	120	120	120
Reserves					
Retained Earnings		-101	-153	-174	-142
Profit or Loss of the Year	-101	-52	-21	32	87
Net Equity	*-51*	*-103*	*-54*	*-22*	*65*
Financial Debts	40	32	24	48	32
Shareholders Account	70	99	44	44	15
Short Term Financial Debts		13	31	5	0
Customers Advances		20	40	55	60
Trade Payables	6	12	19	17	16
Fiscal Liabilities	6	14	25	32	42
Social Contributions and Leave Accruals	20	37	58	72	98
Total Liabilities	92	123	187	252	327

Bibliography

- Taux de survie en 2011 des entreprises créées en 2006 — INSEE
- La France, l'un des pays les plus dynamiques pour les créations d'entreprises — Challenges, 26/07/2013
- Les petites entreprises, créatrices d'emplois. — Le Monde, 31/05/2012
- Panorama de l'évolution des PME — KPMG, 28/06/2012
- Combien d'heures par semaine travaille vraiment votre patron ? — Challenges, 09/10/2013
- Créations et créateurs d'entreprises – Première interrogation 2010, Profil du créateur. — INSEE
- Survey comissioned by CERFRANCE and Novancia for the 21st Salon des Entrepreneurs de Paris. — Institut Think

- Survey wages of entrepreneurs, by company size and industry in 2009 and 2010. — CGPME

- CAC 40 : des effectifs stables en France.
  — Les Echos, 12/11/2013

- Temps partiel dans le secteur de la propreté : L'accord est signé. — FEP (Fédération des Entreprises de Propreté), 13/03/204

- L'impact des seuils de 10, 20 et 50 salariés sur la taille des entreprises françaises. — INSEE, Economie et Statistiques N° 437 – 2010

- Représentation du personnel en entreprise : les seuils sociaux en débat. — Vie Publique, 19/12/2014

- Micro, Small, and Medium Enterprises Around the World: How Many Are There, and What Affects the Count?
  — Word Bank / IFC 2010

- Small companies create 85% of new jobs.
  — EU commission, 16/01/2012

- Global job creation and youth entrepreneurship survey.
  — EY 2015

Acknowledgments

I would like to thank family and friends who encouraged me and contributed to making this project a reality. I would also like to thank the teams I was honored to lead during my 25-year career as well as the CEO's who placed their trust in me, especially at the beginning of my career and who taught me my job...and last but not least the students who inspired me.

A special thanks to Liz Fazenda who helped with the translation of this English edition.

Let's continue our discussion on:

_____

www.mithaetassocies.com

contact@mithaetassocies.com

www.ingramcontent.com/pod-product-compliance
Lightning Source LLC
Chambersburg PA
CBHW070806180526
45168CB00002B/505